Manuela P. Prisco da Cunha

Internet Marketing

Manuela P. Prisco da Cunha

Internet Marketing

The Internet as an Advertising Tool

ScienciaScripts

Imprint
Any brand names and product names mentioned in this book are subject to trademark, brand or patent protection and are trademarks or registered trademarks of their respective holders. The use of brand names, product names, common names, trade names, product descriptions etc. even without a particular marking in this work is in no way to be construed to mean that such names may be regarded as unrestricted in respect of trademark and brand protection legislation and could thus be used by anyone.

Cover image: www.ingimage.com

This book is a translation from the original published under ISBN 978-3-330-77086-7.

Publisher:
Sciencia Scripts
is a trademark of
Dodo Books Indian Ocean Ltd. and OmniScriptum S.R.L publishing group

120 High Road, East Finchley, London, N2 9ED, United Kingdom
Str. Armeneasca 28/1, office 1, Chisinau MD-2012, Republic of Moldova, Europe
Managing Directors: Ieva Konstantinova, Victoria Ursu
info@omniscriptum.com

Printed at: see last page
ISBN: 978-620-8-63397-4

SUMMARY

I dedicate this work to all those who contributed directly or indirectly to its completion, but especially to my parents, who affectionately showed me how necessary study and professional dedication are. I would also like to dedicate this to my husband, who with all his patience has pushed me to pursue my dreams.

I would first like to thank God and my teachers and tutors who helped me to complete this stage in my life.

SUMMARY

Cunha, M. Marketing na Internet: a study on the application of the Internet as an advertising channel used by marketing. Sao José dos Campos, 2010. Monograph. Armando Alvares Penteado Foundation.

This study sought to find out whether the Internet, when used as a channel, a means of advertising communication, developed in accordance with the theories of marketing and its divisions, improves the visibility of Studio Sete Marketing e Design in the eyes of its clients. A non-probabilistic, intentional sample of 6 interviewees was used. The data collection instrument was a script with qualitative questions. The results indicate that the materials developed by Studio Sete Marketing e Design and "applied" to its clients have an effect on their attention and interest.

Keywords: Internet marketing, Internet advertising, Internet relationship between customer and company.

INTRODUCTION

When you think about admitting a channel into the methods used by a particular company to promote its product/service, there's no denying that including the Internet as one of the various marketing tools is a very simplified form, regardless of the sector in which it operates.

To better understand this union, marketing and the Internet, we look at the different ways in which marketing can be explored, such as: strategic, operational and relationship marketing, in each of which the study of the 4Ps should be focused, emphasizing the P of place.

In this respect, it would be interesting to cite the study by Kotler and Keller (2006), where the authors report that Robert Lauterbom suggests that the 4Ps of the salesperson correspond to the 4Cs of the customers, as follows:

4Ps	4Cs
Product Price Square Promotion	Customer (solution for the) Cost (for the customer) Convenience Communication

Source: Kotler and Keller, 2006, p. 17

Figure 01 The 4Ps of the salesperson and the 4Cs of the customer.

With regard to the different types of marketing and their specific objectives, it would be interesting to clarify that:

Strategic marketing seeks to find ways in which the brand or product/service can achieve the expected results. Among these many possibilities, the definition of distribution channels and the development of a coherent and effective form of communication are important points to consider.

As for operational marketing, it is known that this segment is the one that puts into practice the plans defined by strategic marketing, namely: the promotions and advertising campaigns that will be implemented, the actions that will be carried out by salespeople directly at the point of sale, product distribution and merchandising actions, as well as after-sales checks.

Finally, Relationship Marketing, as the name implies, has the function of building long-term and satisfactory relationships for both parties, in order to win and maintain business and partnerships.

The Internet, seen as a communication channel, allows us to think about the possibility of it becoming the "marketplace" for some products / services as well as the "promotion" for some marketing strategies.

In this sense, we sought to follow the work carried out and the results obtained by Studio Sete Marketing e Design, which has been associating the Internet with the company's marketing since it was founded in May of two thousand and seven.

The problem of this project is: Are the techniques used by this company in Internet marketing actions towards its customers in line with what is theoretically cited as interesting to use, and have they obtained any results?

Some of the definite hypotheses as to why this channel is used are:

a) The institutional website effectively increases the company's visibility;

b) Innovative virtual advertising models increase contact between customer and company;

c) The personalization of each material presented to clients increases the degree of affinity with the company.

As a general objective, this work seeks to show the innovation that the Internet brings to the advertising market and whether this is positive or not.

The specific objectives of this work are

a) Compare advertising channels on the internet;

b) Define the benefits of these channels;

c) Evaluate the different audiences that the Internet reaches;

d) Analyze the benefits and facilities of search engines.

With the information taken from the bibliographical research for the theoretical foundation of this project, plus the qualitative field research, carried out after the script had been drawn up and applied to some of Studio Sete Marketing e Design's clients, it was possible to verify the results of using the internet as a publicity channel, as well as the client-studio relationship.

In order to lay the foundations for this work, the first chapter will look at Marketing and its divisions, such as operational, strategic and relationship marketing and, to complement this, it will look at the Internet and its history in the world and in Brazil.

The second chapter will consist of research and case studies related to the project. Firstly, the growth of the internet as a communication channel and advertising in its various forms; secondly, the study of Studio Sete Marketing e Design, its history, its services, its clients and the use of the internet within this company.

Cross-referencing the theoretical information on Internet marketing with the results of the company's field research will lead to a conclusion as to whether or not the aforementioned applications are effective in the market to which Studio Sete belongs, confirming or not the hypotheses raised.

CHAPTER 1 THEORETICAL BACKGROUND

This chapter will present the main issues related to the marketing context of the project in question. Firstly, the conceptual models of the different forms of marketing presentation will be discussed, detailing their functions and characteristics. This will be followed by a look at the beginnings of the Internet, both in the world and in Brazil, in order to finally unite marketing and the Internet.

1 Marketing.

Marketing, in general, is defined as a set of methods and studies that a company uses to include and sustain a product, service or brand in the consumer market. In order for this to happen, it uses a number of promotional methods focusing on its target audience.

According to Kotler and Keller (2006), marketing can lead to the transformation of a particular or social need into a profitable business opportunity and this is basically the principle of marketing; satisfaction in a way that generates profit.

Well-worked and developed marketing results in cautious but also challenging planning and execution.

The placement of marketing in practically every sector of the market has meant that its refinement and reformulations have grown, so that it can serve each company, product or service in an individualized way.

With its dual bases, art and science, it has resulted in a very attractive combination, because even though it generates a tension in managing two opposites, it is possible to include and sustain a company in today's markets by uniting the two aspects of marketing, the formal and the creative.

This requires marketing planning based on factors that cover the entire market scenario in which the company operates, with Swot Analysis being of great importance. This acronym comes from the words strengths, weaknesses, opportunities and threats and, translated into Portuguese, means strengths, weaknesses, opportunities and threats.

This tool is used to analyze and position the company in relation to internal and external factors, in order to see certain details that are fundamental to its success.

Analyzing the strengths and weaknesses within the company makes it possible to assess the situation in which it finds itself and thus choose what to keep and what needs to change. After analyzing the Swot matrix, it is also necessary to study the external factors and their opportunities and threats, relating them to the market in which the company operates.

Once this information is available and has been thoroughly analyzed, it will be possible to establish the strategies to be used by marketing to achieve the four "Ps":

a) Product / Service; that satisfies the customer's needs;

b) Promotion; that communicates and sells to the customer in a diverse way;

c) Price; one that is attractive to the customer and profitable for the company;

d) Square; strategic place to distribute the product / service.

Still within this same principle of the result to be obtained by both parties, two other categories of marketing could be mentioned, as shown below:

> In fact, we can divide marketing in general into two categories: Intrusive and Interactive. The former reaches the consumer, whether they want it or not. This is partly responsible for the torrent of "buy this", "buy that!" papers that a mere mortal receives in their mailbox every day, especially in the USA. This kind of attitude is reprehensible on the net: if you send unsolicited messages to someone's e-mail address, you will probably receive the same message with an addendum referring to you in a less than gracious way (CASTRO, 2000, p. 8).

From the above quote, it is possible to conclude that there is a need for further studies in addition to finding the most appropriate way to use Internet marketing.

To do this, it is essential to investigate each case and each client in order to make good use of the space and the form of communication, so that it achieves its functionality.

1.1 Strategic Marketing.

There are a number of divisions within Marketing, such as Strategic Marketing. This is defined using this name because its functions include strategies for the brand or product/service to achieve the expected results.

As mentioned by Kotler and Keller (2006), there are some functions within marketing such as:

a) Market research

Analyze the market scenario, possible opportunities and threats and how to deal with them.

b) Choice of target audiences

Study who the target audience is, what their needs and desires are and how to meet their expectations.

c) Product/service/brand conception

Developing the product, service or brand according to the needs of the market, analyzing the best way for it to be seen and desired by the public.

d) Setting prices

To set a price, you need to study the market you're in and the financial scenario that the target audience is willing to pay.

e) Defining distribution channels

Strategically observing which sales channels will be the most profitable and give your product, service and/or brand more visibility among your audience.

f) Developing a form of communication

Communication is the way in which the product, service and/or brand will be seen by the market and the public to be reached, so it is necessary to analyze the best form, the most suitable vehicles and the visuals to be used to attract attention and win over customers.

All these functions are essential for the interaction of the market, in which the product/service/brand is contained, with the objectives to be achieved.

Observation and study are important for this area of work within marketing, because each case is different; it is not possible to generalize and use the same techniques and tools for all companies, customization is necessary.

In the case of services, certain needs must be observed when developing marketing strategies, such as:

a) Differentiate yourself in a positive way, creating sympathy for the service and

for the service;

b) Studying the differentials most requested by customers, i.e. checking the

what is missing from the service;

c) Use the provision of some services where the profit margin is

small in order to attract customers to other services, which could bring the company more profit.

1.2 Operational Marketing.

Kotler and Keller (2006) cite yet another extension of the marketing functions; Operational Marketing, which is aimed at operations within the guidelines defined by Strategic Marketing.

This establishes the promotions and advertising campaigns that will be implemented, the direct marketing actions that will be carried out by salespeople at the point of sale, product distribution and merchandising actions. Finally, it is necessary to check after-sales and analyze the results of all the actions taken on the basis of the strategies defined.

For this division of marketing to achieve its objectives, professionals need to be prepared and qualified.

Kotler and Keller (2006) define the marketing professional as follows:

A marketer is someone who seeks a response (attention, purchase, vote, donation) from another party, called a prospect. If two parties are trying to sell something to each other, they are both called marketers

Marketing professionals are trained to stimulate demand for a company's products, but this is a very limited view of the tasks they perform. Just as production and logistics professionals are responsible for managing demand. Marketing managers seek to influence the level, timing and composition of demand in order to meet the organization's objectives (KOTLER and KELLER, 2006, p. 8).

We can therefore conclude that operational marketing is the part where the tasks are carried out, putting into practice everything that was defined in the initial planning and strategies. It can be said, then, that operational marketing is putting the "car" in motion, in order to finally measure the results of the actions.

1.3 Relationship Marketing.

Relationship marketing is another division of marketing as a whole and, as its name implies, its aim is to build links between key parts of a company and the market in which it is located, such as customers, suppliers and other partners who are important for its continuation and growth in the market.

According to Kotler and Keller (2006), relationship marketing refers to cultivating the right kind of relationship with the right group.

Analyzing the context in which the company finds itself, it can be seen that the relationship cannot only be fixed on customers, but also on employees and partners such as channels, suppliers, distributors, resellers and others. In addition, key people within the financial community, such as investors, in order to form a marketing network.

Increasingly, competition is not between companies, but between marketing networks, with the prize going to the company that has built the best network (KOTLER and KELLER, 2006,

p. 16).

The relationship between a company and its customer can begin as a common supplier, among many others that exist. Then it can move on to the position of preferred supplier, which is more segmented and contained in a smaller group, and finally develop a collaborative relationship, in which there is only one supplier for certain customer needs.

The collaborative relationship is based on a closer exchange between supplier and client, with a social connection that goes beyond the business, seeking long-term benefits.

An analysis of the current market shows that relationships are essential for a company to remain profitable and grow, but individualization has become a differential due to lack of time.

A company's ability to deal with each of its customers individually has been made possible by advances in mass customization, computers, the Internet and database marketing software (KOTLER and KELLER, 2006, p. 16).

Customer satisfaction turns out to be extremely important for the life of the company, for example in the case of retail companies where technologies are making it possible for an individualized and lasting relationship between consumer and retailer to take place. This is possible because retailers are trying to solve customer needs more quickly and effectively through database technologies, cultivating customer loyalty and creating a concept of a trusting relationship and quality of service for the consumer.

The interactivity provided by the Internet broadens the concept of relationships to the creation of consumers. (PARENTE, *apud* PORTO, 1999. p. 172-173.).

In order to make the best use of this differential, it is necessary to analyze the wishes and desires of the different groups that make up the marketing network in which the company is inserted. To do this, it is necessary to tailor services and communication individually, while remembering the market's demand for speed.

1.4 The origin of the internet.

The history of the Internet began when four American universities joined together to form a network of laboratories. The purpose of this network was to study the Advanced Research Projects Administration ([1]) of the US Department of Defense, and this project, initially called Arpanet, came to be known in the future as the Internet.

From the union of institutions: University of California, LA and Santa Barbara; Stanford Research Institute; University of Utah and high-tech entrepreneurs; in 1969, researchers and scholars began the project to create the Internet, which lasted throughout the 1970s until the appearance of TCP/IP (Transmission Control Protocol / Internet Protocol).

According to Reedy, Schullo and Zimmerman (2001), Ray Tomlinson of BBN (Bolt Beranek Newman) invented the first email program in 1971, which was used to send messages on the distributed network.

Research continued and in 1972 Larry Roberts, also a researcher, made it possible to selectively use the tools to list, read, archive, send and reply to messages within the email program.

1 Source: <http://www.torque.com.br/internet/historia.htm>. Accessed on 28/08/2008.

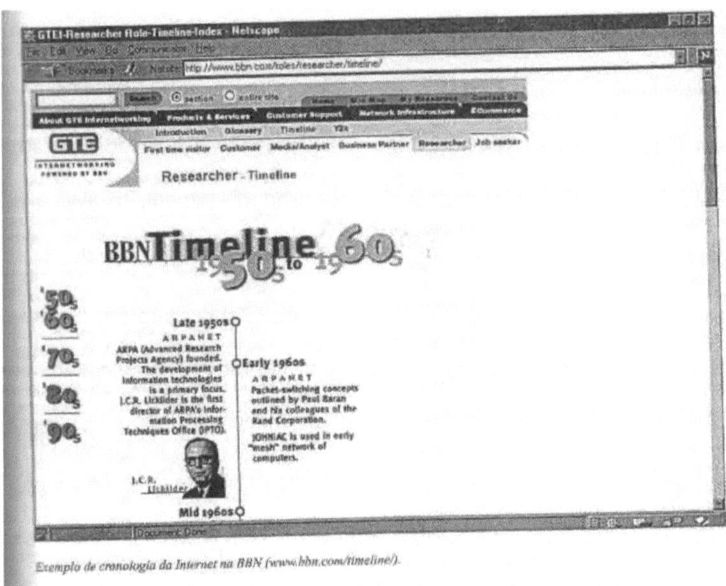

Source: REEDY Joel, SCHULLO Shauna, ZIMMERMAN Kenneth, 2001, p. 101

Figure 02 Example of Internet chronology at BBN ( )www.bbn.com/timeline/

As cited by Reedy, Schullo and Zimmerman (2001), in 1973 Bob Kahn, a researcher at ARPA, started the Internet research program, investigating the techniques and technologies used for networks, with the aim of creating communication protocols with universal standards, so that several computers connected to could exchange information transparently throughout the network.

Kahn continued his research until he arrived at the result of packet switching, where information would be broken down into smaller packets, whether text, image or sound, in order to make the flow of information through the network "lighter", and when the information reached its destination it would be reassembled.

This system has become known over the years as the TCP/IP Protocol Suite, due to the two initial protocols: TCP (Transmission Control Protocol), and IP (Internet Protocol), which are used to connect the main computers to the internet.

All this standardization would lead in the future to the creation of communication applications that would increase precision and speed on the internet, in life and in the job market.

According to Reedy, Schullo and Zimmerman (2001), the first PCs (personal computers) appeared on the market in 1982 and 1983. At this time, an operating system called Berkeley UNIX was used, which included software for networks to facilitate connection to the Internet. This progress continued throughout the 1980s, making computing and the Internet increasingly accessible to the public.

Between 1985 and 1986, the "backbone" of the Internet was developed, known as NSFNET and created by the National Science Foundation (NSF), whose purpose was to connect its computer centers with regional networks, thus generating the Internet.

This technology is still the basis for providing the common language that makes it possible to connect computer networks, enabling and facilitating the transportation of information.

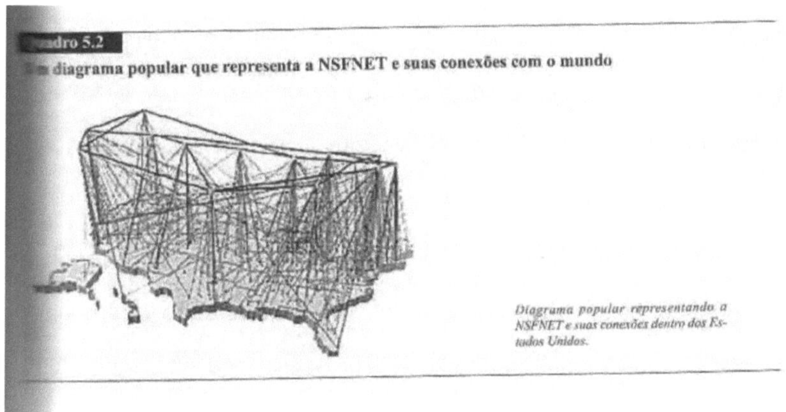

Source: REEDY Joel, SCHULLO Shauna, ZIMMERMAN Kenneth, 2001, P. 101

Figure 03 A popular diagram representing NSFNET and its connections to the world

In 1992, the European Physics Laboratory (CERN) created the World Wide Web (WWW) as a tool for scientists from all over the world to access information. On this network, a million users from various countries such as Cameroon, Cyprus, Ecuador, Estonia, Kuwait,

Luxembourg, Slovakia, Slovenia, Thailand and Venezuela had access to information, and this number rapidly grew.

The Internet went from the status of an academic institution to a commercially exploited area in 1993, when a variety of services began to be provided and opened up worldwide.

Today we can say that the Internet is a large set of computer networks connecting the whole world and enabling the exchange of information and services, regardless of the type and capacity of the users' machines.

1.5 The internet in Brazil.

In Brazil, in 1987, FAPESP (São Paulo State Research Foundation) connected to institutions in the USA (United States of America) and thus had access to international networks, encouraging other organizations to join the Internet as well.

The Internet in Brazil was launched in 1995[2] , when the Ministry of Communications and Science and Technology decided to invest in the implementation of a global Internet network. It had some pre-established concepts such as national coverage, variety in its applications, low cost for the end user and especially for the private sector, thus generating mixed use in the commercial and academic sectors.

In just a decade, the Internet has gone from non-existent to revolutionary in Brazil. In large and small cities, portals such as Terra, Globo, UOL, IG and others are competing for customers and a slice of a totally promising market with prospects for a successful future.

In 2000[3] , Napster, a download site, made it possible for users to share mp3 songs, a fact that sparked a major copyright controversy.

Another major event was the arrival of broadband in Brazil, with the IG portal launching the

2 Source: <http://homepages.dcc.ufmg.br/~mlbc/cursos/internet/historia/Brasil.html>. Accessed on 09/06/2010.
3 Source: <http://www.internetnobrasil.net/index.php?title=2000>. Accessed on 08/06/2010.

first free provider to access the internet.

The explosive development of the Internet, both for academic and commercial use, is becoming more and more visible and everything indicates that it is only going to increase, and with it the number of people connected. This means that more and more different types of services are being offered on the Internet, from buying a product to paying bills and taxes.

This growth is helping more organizations to make themselves visible virtually, be they private companies, governments, NGOs, etc., by creating their own websites and communicating in various ways with their customers, voters and partners, in order to offer their services, products and information.

CHAPTER 2 CASE STUDY RESEARCH

This chapter deals with research into the Internet and its growth as a communication channel for advertising, followed by an analysis of the methods used by Studio Sete Marketing e Design in Internet marketing and their results.

2.1 The growth of the internet.

Communication via the Internet is becoming more technologically efficient by the second, as can be seen from the various ways in which it can reach users.

As seen in the article on the decon.ufpe.br website, in the period from 1985 to April 1994, the Internet grew from 200 networks to over 30,000 and from 1000 hosts to over 2 million hosts[2].

640,000 hosts[4] are educational nodes, 520,000 are commercial nodes, and 220,000 are government/military nodes, while most of the 700,000 or so other nodes are located outside the United States. At the end of 1994, the Internet connected 41,520 networks with approximately 3,864,000 computers (982,000 in American

4 *Host* is the term applied to computers with a web server, which make one or more websites available on the Internet (World Wide Web). Some people also call companies that provide website hosting services, a service also known as "*hosting*".
Source: <http:// www.abc-tecnologia.com.pt/index.php?article=732&visual=1>. Accessed on 05/7/2010.

educational institutions) in 90 countries .[5]

The certainty that the Internet is indispensable nowadays can be confirmed by its great growth in educational and government networks; in addition, it is becoming more and more widespread in electronic commerce and, even though it is still in its infancy, its number of users is increasing daily.

2.2 The origin and growth of Internet advertising.

Advertising on the Internet has become yet another means of communication, with the differential of generating interactivity with its consumers and the great advantage of serving different audiences, from the "masses" to more segmented and elite consumers.

According to the article Mercado e Publicidade online by Missila Loures Cardozo from the Methodist University of Sao Paulo[6] , Internet advertising began in Brazil with the arrival of the Internet in 1994, and the number of Internet users accessing the virtual network has grown.

According to data from IBOPE[7] , the number of residential internet users has reached twenty-five million and almost thirty-three million are connected to the internet in a variety of environments, from home, business, school, etc. As a consequence of this, advertising investment has grown a lot in recent years, so that new advertisers have been using the Internet to publicize their advertising campaigns, as can be seen in the table below.

5 Source: <www.decon.ufpe.br>. Accessed on 25/5/2010.
6 Source: <http://www2.metodista.br/unesco/gcsb/mercado.pdf>. Accessed on 26/2/2010.
7 Source: <http://idgnow.uol.com.br>. Accessed on 24/5/2010.

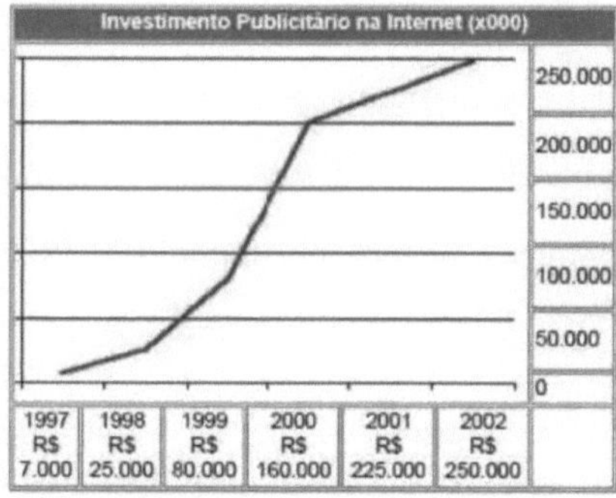

Source: 1997 to 2002 - AMI / 2002 Intermeios

Figure 04 Advertising Investment on the Internet

As a result of this growth, the advertising industry, looking for a new niche market, has been using this vehicle as a great tool, increasing its investments and advertisers every year, displaying campaigns in various spaces on the Internet, or online media, as it is also called.

The great flexibility of this communication vehicle in advertising can be seen in its various divisions, the spaces made available for ads and the technologies used in them.

Some examples of media on the Internet are:

a) Banners: images created in jpg or gif formats or animations such as Java or flash, which can have different sizes and shapes;

b) Interstitial ads: ads produced above the web page, which once seen can be closed by the user with a simple click;

c) Pop-ups: pages that open automatically as soon as you open the site, but there are already blockers to stop them from opening if you don't want them to;

d) Links within articles: links placed within virtual articles so that when the reader clicks on the highlighted word they are sent to a page with the advertisement.

These media can vary according to the technology used to develop the ads, the target audience and their accessibility to Internet users.

The growth of advertising on the Internet has been increasing year on year, as the turnover has also risen, as can be seen in the article "Internet advertising makes 21 billion dollars" on the website www.imasters.uol.com.br[8] . This clearly shows a 25% increase on the 16.9 billion dollars earned in 2006, according to the Interactive Advertising Bureau (IAB) and Pricewaterhouse Coopers (PWC).

It can be seen that the culture of Brazilians when it comes to using the Internet is changing. Currently, the average time Brazilians spend using online services has surpassed that of the United States.

According to Machado (2004) in his article "Propaganda On Demand"[9], Brazilians are sophisticated users who listen to Internet radio, keep in touch with friends, use online government and banking services, look for jobs, etc.

> As the average time spent using the Internet increases, TV begins to lose its audience, according to a survey carried out by the Datanexus Institute in the Greater São Paulo region in January this year. According to the survey, in prime time, between 8pm and 10.30pm, when soap operas monopolize the attention of many, 22% of households without access to the web are watching television, compared to only 15% of those who are plugged in. (MACHADO GILBER, 2004.) .[9]

With this opportunity in mind, advertising invests in approaching a section of the population with great consumer power, some of whom are powerful opinion formers, consumers of novelties and propagators of trends.

The passivity of the other media is leading to the loss of a good slice of the advertising market to what is known as on-demand, in other words, the recipients of the messages sent by the media are becoming more "free" in their desires, determining what they want, when and for how long they want to be exposed to the information broadcast, so they have control over the situation.

8 Source: <www.imasters.uol.com.br>. Accessed on 25/5/2010.
9 Source: < http://webinsider.uol.com.br>. Accessed on 23/5/2010.

Consumer participation and involvement with what is being offered and shown in the media has ceased to be something rare or difficult to access, and has become a consumer demand.

People like to be informed. They like to be kept up to date. They welcome information that they find interesting - but they get bored with uselessness. If your message isn't meaningful to them, it's useless.

Customers generally like to receive industry news, product promotions, useful suggestions and anything that will help them make better use of your products. Stories told by other customers about different ways of using your products, suggestions on how to save time and money are welcome (SETERNE, JIM, 2001, p. 108).

A great proof of this control that consumers are having is the personalization of products and services that are developed directly for someone or some group.

The Internet advertising market is no different. Advertisements are focused on the consumer who, in turn, chooses the way in which they are accessed.

Advertising on the Internet is effective when it manages to arouse the audience's search behavior, seeking, involvement - this is on-demand advertising. The aim is to become part of the digital world, of the target audience, to create moments of positive and unusual digital experience, which are spontaneous advertisements based on viral proliferation on the web. (MACHADO GILBER, 2004). [9].

As Bruner, Harden and Heyman (2001) point out, the Internet has great attractions when it comes to communicating on a global scale. However, most companies don't see that they have in their hands an extremely valuable opportunity for individualized sales, so they end up giving the Internet the image of a technological fish fair, using exaggerated communications and absurd technologies, without focusing on their audience and just using their website as a means of inserting sounds, videos, flashes and lights.

The previous paragraph shows the contrast between communication that focuses on the public and polluting communication that passes no information at all, because it has too much information at the same time. This can be seen in the following paragraph:

Nothing replaces talent, says the advertisement for the contest for the best Brazilian media professionals. This applies much more externally to the web, given the high rate of obsolescence of online advertising, as we have already seen. Thus, an attractive visual becomes the difference between one that will "burn" quickly and another that will never be clicked on! (CASTRO ALVARO, 2000, p. 92).

In short, the above quote shows that the internet should be used well as a medium and that, because it is much wider and easier to access, more people will be able to use it.

2.3 The future of Internet advertising.

As mentioned on the website www.empresasefinancas.hsw.uol.com.br[10] , some professionals who specialize in this subject defend the thesis of the end of traditional advertising on the Internet, because they have observed that the click-through rate on virtual banners has been decreasing with each access by Internet users.

They believe that new forms of advertising are emerging, innovating the way they approach Internet users, such as pop-up ads and windows that appear on their own. These advertisements, which are more popular but disturbing for users who need to close them, lead to a "heavy" load that they place on the site.

Text advertisements contained in a story or piece of information on the site have also been used, and are presented in a non-aggressive and less obvious way to internet users. In addition, interstitial ads, which appear in their own window, are less disturbing to users because they appear first on the site and close by themselves.

It can be seen that Internet advertising tends to grow and innovate, as it is the most important and profitable means for the sustainability of this communication vehicle.

The sale of banner space on the Internet can be done in three different ways: the exchange of space between sites, i.e. one site advertises another's banner on its site and in exchange yours is being advertised; individual posting, when payment is made to for the placement of the banner in the chosen space and, finally, a form well used by advertisers which is network

10 Source: <http://empresasefinancas.hsw.uol.com.br/banners10.htm>. Accessed on 25/5/2010.

posting, organizations that update and post the banner on several registered sites.

This shows the flexibility found within this media, which has room for various types of advertisers and consumers; the only requirement for the ad to have a return is to place the advertisement in the right target (audience).

The web is global, and forgetting your target means that your ad could end up being seen by the Aborigines of Timbuktu. Think about the best time for our target to be surfing, ask the ad host if they can filter it for certain IP classes or something like that. There's little point in advertising to a wide audience if you only intend to deliver locally. All we'll achieve is to create users who are unhappy about having entered our site only to realize that they don't qualify among the privileged who will receive our products. In fact, an example of this is a study published in Iconocast on a banner campaign for the Baby Center website (http://www.babycenter.com). This study showed that campaigns without pronounced targeting generated higher click-through rates at a lower cost per visitor, which should be a good thing. However, this was highly inefficient in terms of sales (CASTRO ALVARO, 2000, p. 96).

Consumers' patience and tolerance for advertisements that waste their time is becoming less and less, or rather zero. They are looking to the internet as a means of speeding up their lives, such as email contact with clients and friends, using home banking sites and e-commerce.

Frequency of Internet Use

The frequency with which you use the internet and the average access time are key factors in its correct use. Studies show that the more internet users surf, the less afraid they are of making *online* transactions, for example. It's good to see that 64% of those interviewed access the web once a day and 70% of them browse for at least an hour each time. The average number of users per computer is around 2.4. This means that for every computer with access to *nvl*>, we can count on at least 2 users.

	Nov./96	Aug./97	Aug./98
More than once a day	44%	43%	44%
Once a day	21%	21%	20%-
Several times a week.	31%	33%	31%
Several times a month	4%	3%	2%

Source: Castro, Âlvaro, Propaganda e media digital A web como a grande media do presente, ano 2000 p.17.

Figure 05 Frequency of Internet Use

According to the previous survey, we can see the high frequency and the high level of access that internet users are having to the internet; this confirms and reinforces the power that advertising can have by using this media in its campaigns.

As a result, innovation and the search for sites that provide advertisers with the flexibility, interactivity and personalization of the web are growing by the second.

A sound website probably exploits many, if not all, of the following attributes. The best web architecture is:

- Interactive
- Staff
- Infocentric
- Instant
- Measurable
- Flexible
- Interconnected
- Economic.

(BRUNER, RICK E. / HARDEN, LELAND / HEYMAN, BOB, 2001, p. 50).

Companies that pay attention to these items will be one step ahead of their competitors, because with the global market, it is unacceptable for a potential customer not to be able to find out about a company's product via the web, as this form of research is already widespread in the minds of today's consumers and will be increasingly so in the future.

In an increasingly global market, it's perfectly possible that the only way a potential customer can discover a company's product is through cyberspace, and for many companies that's reason enough to be there. Awareness also has a tangible value in the equity value of the brand when a company is merged or sold (BRUNER, RICK E. / HARDEN, LELAND / HEYMAN, BOB, 2001, p. 28, 29).

2.4 Web, trap or opportunity for advertising?

The Internet, like any other media, can be the big boom for a brand or a big fiasco. This result depends not so much on the vehicle, but much more on the marketing strategy drawn up by the professionals.

The Internet, being a medium that can reach many different types of audiences, ends up being undervalued in terms of its strength. Many advertisers, because they don't believe that the web can be an essential medium for strengthening their brand, overlook a very important fact: studying the marketing strategies that should be used, such as which sites to advertise on, which spaces to buy, which internet users access these chosen sites and what their financial return would be.

Another fact that often ends up "devaluing" the influence of the web on campaigns and ads is its low cost. However, this lack of credibility should be focused on the incorrect use of funds, i.e. on unsuitable sites and spaces. This leads to ads that don't reach the target consumer, brand wear and tear due to not being able to supply the consumer who had access to the ad, as well as financial loss, since the focus is not on the product on offer.

The Web can be a cost-effective arm of all a company's marketing efforts, or it can be a real money-losing trap if the company doesn't have a clear and measurable marketing objective in mind. Each company's business goals depend on different factors, but the majority of successful online ventures, even those that don't have a direct commercial function, have a clear and measurable marketing goal.

believes that the Internet offers marketers an RSI in one of the following ways:

- Brand solidification
- Generating sales prospects
- Online sales
- Customer support
- Market research
- Publication of content.

(BRUNER, RICK E. / HARDEN, LELAND / HEYMAN, BOB, 2001, p. 27).

The great advantage of the internet is its agility and interactivity, which directly helps to establish a brand, especially if it is new to the market.

With interactivity, the web differs from other media in that it allows its consumers or potential consumers to come into direct contact and get involved with the company and its products as many times a day as they wish. This is due to the fact that there are no obstacles or paths to follow to the company, since it is in front of its audience's eyes without any physical effort, which makes it easier for them to request services, delve into product details and contact it whenever and however they want.

Another great advantage is its agility, which makes it an ally for advertisers or marketing professionals who need a means of communication that provides flexibility and speed.

Although the Web makes it easier to keep a product's name in front of the right audience, many advertisers are looking for more immediate results than brand awareness. For such marketers, the Web is paradise (BRUNER, RICK E. / HARDEN, LELAND / HEYMAN, BOB, 2001, p. 30).

It can therefore be seen that the best way for virtual advertising to work is to combine virtual technology and marketing, because only with these two tools in hand will you be able to do a great job and take advantage of all the opportunities that the Internet offers.

2.5 Studio Sete Marketing and Design.

Studio Sete cannot be defined as an advertising agency, since it has a different structure to them.

Its definition is Studio, as it comes from the word estùdio, which according to Dicionârio Novo Aurélio - O Dicionârio da Lingua Portuguesa: S.m 1. Ateliê (2) 2. Place suitable for filming,

recordings for radio and television, sound recordings in general, etc. 3. a place for other artistic activities such as dance and theater classes, screenings of selected shows or films, etc. (FERREIRA, 1999, p. 846).

Studio Sete Marketing e Design is a mix between an artistic workshop and advertising and publicity, as it provides services in the creation of art and projects to publicize products, services or brands.

Its structure began in May 2007, but its origins go back years, when its creator was already working in the creative field in advertising and publicity in mid-2002. Even as an employee at other agencies, she was already freelancing for other clients under the pseudonym Studio Sete.

For its real launch on the Sâo José dos Campos market, it was necessary to look for bases and information and, in March 2007, it began searching for ways to be able to have some security in its investments in this dream.

After a survey of what would be needed to make these plans a reality, in May of that year he began to set up a office in the Jardim Augusta neighborhood of São José dos Campos and began to advertise his services to his old and new clients.

After a year of work, new clients were won over and the range of services improved.

2.5.1 Services provided by Studio Sete Design.

According to the board of directors in informal conversations, Studio Sete Marketing e Design provides services in the areas of web design, graphic art, visual identity and multimedia, which can be defined as:

a) Web design - creation and development of websites, webmails, advertisements and virtual projects;

b) Arte Gràfica - creation and development of printed materials for advertising such as folders, billboards, pamphlets, magazines, advertisements, etc;

c) Visual identity - study and creation of logos and stationery;

d) Multimedia - development of interactive materials such as interactive CDs and DVDs, presentations and animations.

Among the services provided, Studio Sete's focus is on web design, which is not only the most dynamic but also the most cost-effective, analyzing the cost benefit and time spent on development.

One of its great benefits is its reusability. Advertising a product in a promotion on a website means that when it ends or the date of the promotion expires, the work doesn't need to be discarded, whereas if it were printed material, if the distribution wasn't complete, the rest would be lost.

2.5.2 Clients served by Studio Sete Marketing e Design and services provided.

Below are some of the clients Studio Sete Marketing e Design has served and the work it has done for them:

Instituto Odontológico Adhemar Prisco, a company in the oral health sector, where professionals such as dentists from different specialties practice. For this client, a yogo-brand and a visual identity manual were initially developed, with the aim of creating the "face" of this company. To continue the visual communication work, an institutional website was also developed, which facilitates communication between dentist and patient and, finally, internal identification materials were developed to integrate the patient into the environment.

As a way of maintaining these aforementioned investments, an informative webmail is periodically developed with interesting and important information, sent via e-mail to patients.

Instituto Dr. Newton Roberto Ribeiro, a company also in the field of dentistry, for which the following projects were developed: institutional website, informative webmails to update patients and partners on news in the field and from professionals, advertisements for printed media and an interactive CD to present treatments to patients and partners in the office.

Dental Clinic, dental clinic; client for whom the institutional website was developed with information about the professionals, the clinic and about treatments and tips for patients' oral health.

Laboratório de prótese Mendrot & Mendrot provides laboratory services for dentists and other oral health professionals. An institutional website was developed for this group of professionals.

W&E Representações e Vendas is in the field of home products, such as bathroom enclosures, mosquito nets, protective screens, gates and more. For this client, the institutional website containing its portfolio was first developed, followed by a hot site and webmail to publicize the company's participation in the Lar Doce Lar program on Rede Globo's Caldeirâo do Huck.

Equatorial Sistemas, a company operating in the space technology market, created a website with institutional content and an online news service. This was followed by relationship marketing work, with the creation of commemorative virtual cards to send to clients and partners.

Monteiro Lobato City Hall; a client for whom a new, more up-to-date and complete website has been developed, which is updated weekly with news and useful information for residents and tourists. At the same time, visitation reports are analyzed using the Google Analytics tool, in order to visualize the frequency of visitors, length of time spent on the site and on certain content, geographical origin of visitors and other extremely important information for analyzing the audience being reached and what they are looking for.

Sigecon is a company active in the condominium management market and for it we developed all the flash animations within the site that already existed and was being reformulated.

Geman Engenharia is in the civil construction sector and the following projects were developed for the company: the institutional website; a hot site for the "Il Terrazzo" project, which is updated monthly with images showing the progress of the work and financial control data; the modernization of the logo and its identity manual; banners and signs for external identification of the works; the company's institutional folder and informative webmail to send to clients and partners.

Control Print works in the graphics sector and Studio Sete Marketing e Design provides services for this company, developing graphic and virtual materials, updating the website, which was also created by the Studio, and developing flyers and virtual cards for to maintain the relationship between company, client and partners.

Trimec Esquadrias is a retailer of aluminum frames. For this company, an institutional website was created and the Google Analytics report was used to observe the frequency of visits.

Embratex engenharia, this client is in the civil engineering market and in order to gain wider visibility they developed a website featuring their services and what they are all about. To this end, pages with explanatory videos were inserted, showing how each type of service is carried out and the tools they use.

Stilo Movelaria, in the planned furniture segment. For this client, an extended communication project was carried out, with a redesign of the website and other internal and external materials such as stationery, folders, pamphlets, etc., as well as a whole planning and application of relationship marketing between the furniture store and its customers.

Arantes Marmoraria, a company that works with marble and decorative stones, created a new logo and the company's entire visual identity; internal materials such as stationery, business cards and internal identification; as well as external materials such as folders, pamphlets and institutional webmail sent to clients.

Visótica, a client in the photography and optics market, whose work was based on the creation of promotional materials such as banners and tarpaulins for the façade with promotions; updates to the website with the inclusion of the same information virtually and also printed materials such as guarantee certificates.

2.5.3 Internet as a tool for publicizing Studio Sete Marketing e Design's clients.

Studio Sete Marketing Design uses the Internet as a means of communicating its clients to consumers.

The methods of dissemination used via the internet are:

a) Corporate website;

b) Promotional hot sites;

c) Webmail;

d) Online newsletters;

e) Visitation studies using Google analytics;

f) Registration on search engines;

g) Advertisements on regional websites;

Among others.

The aim of these materials is to provide a weekly or monthly reminder of the existence and permanence of Studio Sete's clients in the market, as well as to publicize the services provided and the promotions that are taking place. The use of this tool also applies mainly to its almost minimal cost and its agility in reaching the end consumer in a matter of minutes.

These methods of promotion are also widely used in the Studio's own marketing to its clients, as they provide a frequent and intense relationship and also end up influencing them in the use and results of these for their companies.

2.6 Scenery.

Studying the case of Studio Sete Marketing e Design and its methods of using internet marketing to advertise its services to clients, a study was carried out with the aim of observing the results of what is being presented by this Studio in its use of the internet as a marketing strategy tool.

Within this objective, a number of items were analyzed:

a) Comparison of the tools used;

b) Definition of advantages and disadvantages;

c) Evaluation of customer feedback;

d) Comparison of the use of phone books and search engines;

e) Evaluation of what is being presented by the market that is not used in the Studio and requested by clients.

The analysis of these items was based on bibliographical research, carried out through books, websites and magazines, as well as field research, the latter developed through the application of a script, within the qualitative exploratory methodology, seeking to analyze each client individually.

2.7 Research.

The field research was carried out using a non-probabilistic, intentional sample with 06 interviewees.

The script was applied in individual interviews, using places and times pre-defined between the interviewee and the interviewer. In some cases, email was used to send the interview, and after the interviewee had given his thoughts over the phone, he sent his answers in the same way. The aim was to make the interviewee as comfortable as possible in order to obtain more truthful information.

The model of the script used can be found in the project's appendix.

2.8 Results.

With the questions individually analyzed, the following results are obtained:

In the question, what service does Studio Sete Marketing e Design provide for your company, each interviewee described the work they have already done with the Studio, such as: logos, printed and virtual promotional materials and websites.

In a second question, the interviewees mentioned which methods Studio Sete used to advertise its services and, at this point, we began to analyze what the interviewees remembered receiving as "advertisements" from the Studio.

In this regard, it can be seen that all the interviewees mentioned two types of email marketing: news about the work they had done and commemorative dates. Some of them said they were satisfied with the Studio's "reminder" of special dates.

The clients also mentioned that they had been sent a questionnaire to remind them that their company's website could be changed and that it was important to keep it up to date, but they didn't mention the institutional website. In this respect, when asked personally by the interviewer if they had already accessed it, few said they had, and those who had done so had done so via the links in the marketing emails.

When asked about the significance of the methods mentioned above, the responses were very diverse. Some said that the questionnaire speeds up communication and reminds them of the need to update the company's website; others referred to email marketing with news and special dates, because it made them feel important and remembered, as well as demonstrating that relationship marketing can bring company and customer closer together, as well as being a simple, easy and inexpensive method.

After evaluating the advertising methods that Studio Sete used with the interviewees, they were asked whether or not their contact with them had allowed them to see the need to use them in their companies. All the clients were interested and some had already introduced them in their companies and others would like to include these materials in their communications. One of them specifically claimed that, as well as using email marketing and frequent updates on his website, he had already been congratulated by clients on his work and asked who developed it and how it worked.

When asked what improvements could be made to Studio Sete's communication with clients, most of them said that they would like to have communication that could guide them on the best ways to advertise to their market and their audience, believing that there was a need for newsletters with this specific information.

At the end of the survey, we asked about Studio Seven's definition of the interviewee's company in relation to the methods they mentioned. There were a variety of answers, from not knowing the company in depth because they had only been working for a short time, to the fact that they believe in these methods and find them interesting because they speed up their day-to-day work, not forgetting the fact that they are especially remembered by partners.

CHAPTER 3 DISCUSSION

This chapter contains all the observations, criticisms, suggestions and options for improvement to be proposed to Studio Sete Marketing e Design, with the aim of increasingly developing its performance in relation to its clients through internet marketing, and to keep their memories of the studio "on".

As has been discussed throughout the work, more specifically in Chapter 2, there are several variables that influence Internet marketing. Analyzing the environment, the consumer market and Internet marketing, based on what was found through research and cited by Machado (2004), the use of the Internet as a channel for advertising has increased and both consumers and advertisers have paid attention to the important points for successful Internet advertising, which are:

a) Analysis of the environment: advertisers and internet users identify internet marketing as a great tool for everyone, helping with the speed and agility that everything requires, but they see opportunities for improvement. The strong point of this segment is its agility, but there is still distrust due to the countless "fake" advertisements that people receive on a daily basis.

b) Analysis of the consumer market: Internet marketing can be used in different ways, because the Internet is a means of communication that encompasses different types of audiences and, in order to use it correctly as a marketing tool, it is necessary to create strategies that are more focused on the result you want to achieve. One example is the use of email marketing by companies to send their customers and partners the news they want to share; this is a form of advertising that can be good or not, depending on how it is done and who it is sent to because, nowadays, people don't open emails from people they don't know for fear of viruses or just spam.

However, if it is sent to the right people and in the way they expect, it will be a means of communicating with consumers and could even become something that attracts attention and creates a relationship between company and customer.

By analyzing the 4 "Ps" and 4 "Cs" of marketing at Studio Sete Marketing e Design, as cited by Kotler and Keller (2006), the following considerations can be made:

Product: Studio Sete Marketing e Design's product is advertising services, the creation of printed and virtual materials, as well as marketing plans for what its clients need. The main way of publicizing its portfolio is through its website.

Client: the service that the Studio offers its clients enables solutions in the form of publicizing its products or brand, generating awareness of it among consumers and, ultimately, generating the profit that the company needs to survive in the market.

Price: the prices for these services vary greatly because no job is the same as another, so each project is quoted taking into account what will have to be done, how it will be developed and how long it will take to complete.

Cost: there are two types of client: innovators and entrepreneurs who know the importance of promoting their brand, and those who think that this type of service can be done in any way, without any professionalism. In the first case, the value is an investment that will return to the company in the form of profits in the future; in the second case, it's just a cost, and they don't see these services as something that will strengthen the brand so that it can remain in the increasingly competitive market.

Marketplace: the Internet is a marketplace for the Studio, a "place" for advertising. It is here that its services and the work it does are publicized so that everyone can have access to them, plus the indispensable tool of email, which is used not only to exchange information but also to build relationships with clients.

Convenience: for customers, convenience is the biggest attraction. Anything that can make communication and daily tasks easier is well accepted, and people don't opt for services and products that don't have this "differential". As a result, the internet has been largely responsible for bringing this convenience to people's lives, so that they don't even have to leave the house to buy a takeaway, go to the bank or keep in touch with friends, clients and professional partners.

Promotion: Studio Sete is a company that offers advertising as one of its services; however, it is still a company and needs to promote itself through a website, promotional materials, advertisements and more. Because of this need, it uses strategic planning to focus on its target audience and uses and abuses its knowledge of easy, low-cost "advertisements".

Communication: what customers want is to be communicated with, whether they are the communicator or the receiver of the message. This is because the only way to sell products and make brands grow in the market is to advertise; to communicate what you are selling to your consumers and potential customers.

With regard to the subject studied, Studio Sete Marketing e Design, what can be evaluated is that the methods used by its clients as a form of communication, email marketing and the website, are seen in a positive light and this, also observed by Seterne (2001), generates interest for use in the communication of their companies.

The vast majority of customers interviewed said they were interested in receiving marketing emails, because they keep them up to date and remind them of what can be done to promote the company, with the aim of increasing the relationship with their customers.

Not all clients saw the Studio's communication as an advertisement; some of them reported that they felt "loved" when they received an email congratulating them on a special date, such as Mother's Day or Father's Day, among other dates worked on by the Studio.

By analyzing the previous paragraphs, we can see how important this tool is for the Studio and then see what can be improved.

One difficulty encountered in the customer survey was access to the Studio's website. Few clients accessed the site in an attempt to see what new work had been developed or what was new in the advertising area; few reported entering the site, and these only accessed it when they received the marketing email with a direct link to the site, by clicking on the image that appeared in the email.

To conclude the discussion, it was possible to observe during the research that, once the Internet has been used on the basis of Strategic Marketing, creating and planning actions to publicize Studio Sete in a way that suits its needs, and using the marketing functions cited by Kotler and Keller (2006), the result is success in Relationship Marketing. In this way, "bonds" are cultivated correctly and with the target audience, in other words, there is personalization and individualization between Studio Sete and the client.

CONCLUSION

The results of this monograph show that Studio Sete Marketing e Design's clients positively accept the communication it provides; however, they still feel a certain need for more focused communication in order to inform them, not just about the Studio's portfolio or commemorative dates, but also about something that will benefit their company, generating possible profits or reducing costs.

Comparing the information gathered in the bibliographical research with that obtained from the script applied to some of the Studio's clients, the following conclusions can be drawn:

In the first hypothesis, the objective was to check whether the institutional website effectively increases the company's visibility. Looking at the results obtained in the survey, it was possible to see that in the case of Studio Sete, the institutional website does not attract the attention of its clients to use it as a way of searching for new opportunities within the company's advertising. This means that it only serves new clients who are looking for the service on the internet and are looking for a communications company to develop this service, making it easier for the client to view their portfolio for analysis.

The second hypothesis stated that innovative virtual advertising models increase contact between customers and companies. This was confirmed, as it was found that customers are "open" to news and information that comes to them in the right way.

As an example of customers' acceptance of differentiated advertising, we can cite the response given by one of them stating that they use communication tools such as email marketing with news and information for their customers, as well as useful updates for their consumers such as news about the market, and promotions, actions which have a positive impact on their customers and partners.

Studio Sete's website has not been updated to make it more attractive to its clients. It is suggested that this site should take into account the needs of Internet users looking for the

Studio's site and the information that its clients need and that could be found on it.

The third hypothesis stated that personalizing each piece of material presented to customers increases the degree of affinity with the company. This was confirmed during the research, when it was found that customers are looking for forms of communication that add their company to their daily lives.

However, it was found that there is a lack of personalization in the communication materials used by Studio Sete, since it uses generalized communication with its clients, who, being from different market areas, see communication and internet marketing in different ways.

Based on this study, it can be concluded that there is a great need for personalization of Internet marketing and, with this, consumer demand for the advertisements they receive by email or via the Internet, through websites, is growing, as is their intolerance of unhelpful emails and websites that are not interesting and responsive.

It is suggested that Studio Sete Marketing e Design pay attention to the real needs of its clients and adapt its forms of communication to them. In addition, it is necessary to create strategies to win over consumers in a personalized way, including in its marketing the use of the Internet, advertisements that attract the attention of its customers individually or separated by market sectors, such as health, commerce, food and others.

BIBLIOGRAPHICAL REFERENCES

BRUNER, Rick, HARDEN, Leland, HEYMAN, Bob. Online Marketing Strategies, Best Practices and Case Studies. Sao Paulo: Futura, 2001

CASTRO, Alvaro. Propaganda e media digital A web como a grande media do presente, Rio de Janeiro: QualityMark, 2000

FERREIRA, Aurélio, Novo Aurélio - O dicionàrio da Lingua Portuguesa, Rio de Janeiro: Nova Fronteira, 1999.

KOTLER, Philip and KELLER, Kevin L., Marketing Management The Marketing Bible. Sao Paulo: Prentice Hall Brazil, 2006

PARENTE, Juracy. Retail in Brazil: management and strategy. Sao Paulo: Atlas, 2000.

REEDY, Joel, SCHULLO, Shauna, ZIMMERMAN, Kenneth. Electronic marketing: integrating electronic resources into the marketing process. Porto Alegre: Bookman, 2001

STERNE, Jim. Customer Service on the Internet, Sao Paulo: Makron Books, 2001

WEBGRAPHIES

ABC-TECHNOLOGY - www.abc-tecnologia.com.pt/index.php?article=732&visual=1

INTERNETNOBRASIL - http://www.internetnobrasil.net/index.php?title=2000

METHODIST - http://www2.metodista.br/unesco/gcsb/mercado.pdf

TORQUE - http://www.torque.com.br/internet/historia.htm

UFMG - http://homepages.dcc.ufmg.br/~mlbc/cursos/internet/historia/Brasil.html

UFPE - www.decon.ufpe.br

UOL - http://empresasefinancas.hsw.uol.com.br/banners10.htm

UOL - http://idgnow.uol.com.br

UOL - http://webinsider.uol.com.br

UOL - www.imasters.uol.com.br

APPENDIX

Customer survey script:

1. Name:

2. Company:

3. Function:

4. What kind of services does Studio Sete Marketing e Design provide for your company?

5. What kind of methods does Studio Sete Marketing e Design use to promote its services to your company?

6. Which of these methods is most significant for your company?

7. What is your view of these methods?

8. Have any of them made your company use similar methods to publicize its services?

9. What do you think could be done to improve communication between Studio Sete Marketing e Design and your company?

10. Define Studio Seven Marketing and Design for your company in relation to the methods used to communicate with your company via the internet?

Printed by Books on Demand GmbH, Norderstedt / Germany